A MORE COMPLETE BEAST

JACK DONOVAN

DISSONANT HUM
CASCADIA

FIRST PAPERBACK EDITION

ISBN 13: 978-0-9854523-7-7
ISBN 10: 0-9854523-7-4

Cover and Interior Artwork and Design by Jack Donovan.

Published by Jack Donovan and Brutal Company, LLC.

DISSONANT HUM
An Imprint of Brutal Company, LLC.
2149 CASCADE AVE STE 106A BOX 307
HOOD RIVER, OR 97031-1087

www.jack-donovan.com

Subjects:

1. Social Sciences - Men's Studies
2. Psychology - Men
3. Men - Social Conditions
4. Philosophy
5. Gender Studies
6. Sex Role

CONTENTS

For reactionaries...

PREFACE

The ideas in this book were introduced in a speech titled, "A More Complete Beast" that I delivered at the 21 Convention in Orlando, Florida in 2017. I'm proud of that speech, and 21 Studios released a video recording of it which is currently available online. I'd encourage anyone reading this to watch that speech as the best and most dynamic possible introduction to this book.

A More Complete Beast is dedicated to reactionary men, and presents my solutions to many chronic problems I noticed while traveling in various reactionary circles over the years. The biggest problem with reactionaries is that they are always reacting — always taking a conservative, defensive position, always losing a war of attrition against forces of change, instead of becoming creative forces of change and innovation themselves. All they do is throw out jabs while stepping backward. They struggle with and are stymied by resentment and hatred. I see Nietzsche's thoughts on "ressentiment," "master morality," and "nobility" as philosophical tools they can employ to overcome this reactionary negativity and begin moving forward again. Only by moving forward can they become more like the great men of the past whom they admire.

You'll get even more out of this book if you read the first essay in Nietzsche's *A Genealogy of Morals*, then *Beyond Good and Evil*, *Thus Spoke Zarathustra*, and *The Birth of Tragedy*. In that order. You don't need them to understand this book, but they are worth reading.

However, you won't understand what I mean when I talk about masculinity — much less "The Empire of Nothing" — unless you read my books *The Way of Men* and *Becoming a Barbarian*.

As a formatting note, after checking various translations of Nietzsche's work against the original German, I saw the value of numbering sections and passages. Several of my books have already been translated, and I don't know why people stopped doing that. It makes finding thoughts and quotations much easier. So I have numbered sections of this book, mostly to identify natural breaks and transitions of thought.

I realize that Nietzsche was anti-Christian, and many Christians will find these ideals unreconcilable with Christian ideals. However, while as a pagan the how's and why's are of little interest to me personally, I do believe that what lies ahead will still be of interest to my many Christian readers. We face many similar challenges.

Finally, if this book leaves you wanting more, that is by design. This is an argument for overcoming ressentiment and   for taking a more creative approach to life — not a guide or a "how-to." This book is a transitional spring forward to the next thing. My next project will be "a journal of becoming" — a themed, magazine-style compilation of essays, interviews, artwork and photography published two or three times a year.

START THE WORLD!

Jack Donovan
Cascadia, North America

A MORE COMPLETE BEAST

"At the commencement, the noble caste was always the barbarian caste: their superiority did not consist first of all in their physical, but in their psychical power—they were more complete men (which at every point also implies the same as 'more complete beasts')..."

Friedrich Nietzsche, *Beyond Good and Evil*

Absolute masculinity is a lodestar in the human mind—an untouchable navigational point indicating the farthest imaginable distance along a particular longitude mapping the way that men, as beasts, conceptualize their world. It represents a perfect form—the "most masculine"—a cluster of physical, behavioral and spiritual qualities that, in their most extreme expression, differentiate human males from human females.

The Way of Men leads toward this flickering and elusive point of absolute masculinity. This path of conflict, this never-ending challenge to demonstrate strength, courage and mastery, to win and defend honor, is a product of human evolution. Human masculinity is a hypertrophic development of the body and psyche in response to external pressure— to the looming threats of predation, intergroup conflict, environmental stress, and resource scarcity. In the absence of external pressure, masculinity either fails to develop in the first place, or slowly atrophies.

When people wonder if the men of their age are less manly — farther from the "most-masculine" — than the men who preceeded them, this absence of development is generally explained by a corresponding absence of pressure.

2

Within the boundaries of The Empire of Nothing, most men experience very few of the survival pressures that shaped the masculinity of our ancestors.

The primary role of a man has always been to fight to defend or expand the perimeter of his group's control, to build and maintain an ordered world within that perimeter, to venture beyond the warmth and safety of its nuclear fires to secure necessary resources — and to hunt and kill animals to feed his people.

Today, hunting is a luxury, not a necessity. It's an expensive hobby. No man needs to hunt game for a living. He can purchase farmed meat, killed by strangers, far more easily and in most cases in exchange for fewer assets.

A good citizen of the Empire need not venture far to secure the resources necessary for his own survival or the survival of his dependents. There is no dangerous unknown he must travel through. He travels public transit or drives a car down well-travelled roads and highways to work in offices and factories and stores, in most cases performing tasks that could be done better by a machine if it were more cost effective. The only dangers he faces are social dangers — the threat of being accused of some trending moral infraction by ambitious nihilists, self-aggrandizing shrews or their shrinking cuckold yes-ma'ams.

Even this job-hunting is in many cases only necessary as a matter of tenuous custom. To those unconcerned by the withering social disgrace associated with collecting government assistance, a pauper's leisure can be ensured for a lifetime by submitting the proper forms. This appealing grift need only be interrupted by provisional periods of symbolic employment.

The role of men has always been to deal with violence, but the majority of men living well outside of "failed state" no-go zones will never experience the threat of real violence from anyone but the police — to whom they have outsourced their roles unwittingly, helplessly and without consent. The bodies of citizens are continuously scanned by an unknowable number of surveillance cameras designed to deter or prosecute acts of interpersonal civilian violence. A Byzantine and equally unknowable system of laws regulate every aspect of human existence. The streets and highways are swarming with law enforcement officers who restlessly issue petty citations as they wait for opportunities to cuff up any real or perceived threat to public safety and shuffle offenders through corrupt courts into concrete memory holes.

The state isn't a threat that you can "fight off" in the way a man would fight off a raiding clan. Few of the same principles or tactics apply to protecting yourself against it. All of the strength, courage, mastery and honor in the world are irrelevant in this conflict. When the red eye in the sky locks in on a target, it will just keep sending more drones until even the best men are overwhelmed and subdued. This sense of utter futility helps many men rationalize their undeveloped virility as a way of making peace with powerlessness. *Why bother?*

3

The argument made most frequently by those who have something to gain by encouraging men to allow themselves to become weaker, more passive and more sedentary — state agencies, entertainment and luxury marketers, and of course feminists — is that the tactical virtues associated with male tribal strength culture are no longer necessary. That, in fact, masculinity is no longer necessary. And...*they are correct.*

Masculinity is now optional. If you are an adult male living and working within the boundaries of this globalized commercial police state, no one is forcing you to test yourself against other men. No one is forcing you to become stronger than you already are, effortlessly, as a random product of genetics and circumstance. In most cases people would prefer that you simply relax. Your irritating obsession with self-realization will just make everyone else uncomfortable.

While it is possible that you may find yourself in a situation where you will have to step up and be a man, it is more likely that you won't — and entirely possible that if you do, you may well be penalized for it.

Men who spend no time training the metaphorical muscle of masculinity like to believe that they would be able to step in and be a hero if some extreme scenario demanded it, but this is for the most part a fantasy sold to them by the entertainment industry. Men who work in call centers and spend all of their free time watching television or playing video games are not going to fight off any man who has experience with violence. They're not going to save the world, or their girlfriends, or even themselves.

Many advocates of masculinity, especially self-defense instructors, recognize this reality and ask, "why would you want to be that guy who is helpless and utterly dependent in an emergency?" No man is truly comfortable thinking of himself this way.

However, while it is always better to be prepared than it is to be unprepared, most men who do nothing will be fine. Nothing is going to happen to them. The statistics favor the lazy. Men today are free to be weak and afraid and inept in all of the ways that their ancestors were not.

Those who say that masculinity is no longer necessary are correct.

Those who say that circumstances no longer require the average man to be stronger than the average woman are correct.

Those who say that average men don't need to be any more courageous than average women are correct.

There is no particular set of skills that average men need to acquire more than average women in order to survive.

Honor, the fourth tactical virtue, is dead in any broad cultural sense, so maintaining a commitment to some antiquated honor code that most people don't recognize or value — let alone adhere to — is perceived as being quaintly eccentric, if not "problematic" or threatening in some abstract way.

4

While it is true that masculinity is not necessary — that it is not needed or required of most men by society and they don't need it to survive — to say that the pursuit of masculinity should be abandoned *because* it is not necessary is merely an argument from *utility*. The utilitarian argument against masculinity presupposes that the only legitimate reasons for living, behaving and acting in a particular way are either that one is forced to do so by external circumstances, or coerced to do so by a group. If you accept this argument, you accept that you believe it is *most* important to you to be *useful*.

But, useful to whom? To humankind? To "society," whatever that means? And if so, what are the goals of this society that demands your usefulness? Do you you even know? What are its boundaries and defining beliefs? What is its *telos*? Where is it going? Why are you helping? Are you merely a *useful*...idiot? To merely want to be useful — this is highest value of a man who has resigned himself to the life of a slave.

"How may I be of service, master?"

This is, of course, the human norm. Keep your head down and at least make yourself useful, so that no one will bother you. Shut up and do what you're told and you'll get your promised pittance and pussy.

In the Empire of Nothing, defined by its cosmopolitain commercialism and its institutionalized hatred of exclusive identities, to be a good citizen and a good man is to extend what might have been your reciprocal commitment to family, tribe or nation to every living, breathing human being on the planet. To place yourself in the service of everyone, everywhere. Billions of total strangers. And if we are to owe everyone everything, we really don't owe anyone a damn thing.

We no longer live in traditional societies or caste societies. Most of us have no "people" beyond our immediate families. Our purpose is not predetermined. We are free to choose our purpose, and if we so chose, to offer our service freely.

Tools are useful. I am a man. I am not alive to be useful. I'm alive to live and to thrive.

I am not a slave. If you want me to do what you believe is necessary — convince me that it is also in my best interest, or bargain with me, or make me an offer I can't refuse. I'm not going to change who I am or invert my own values because someone, somewhere — some stranger theorizing about what is "necessary" for society — tells me to, while offering me absolutely nothing of value to me in return.

Great men are not remembered for being prudent or for doing what they were told was necessary. They are remembered for going above and beyond what is merely necessary for survival. Great men are remembered for decisive vision and daring action. They are remembered for founding new orders, building new worlds around themselves, and creating great beauty.

Utility is a god for desiccated souls. It's a baseline. A bare minimum standard. It's what you settle for. It's "good enough."

Great men are not motivated by what is necessary, satisfactory or practical. Great men are motivated by what is...great. That which is necessary merely facilitates beauty and greatness.

Masculinity is no longer necessary. Today, masculinity is a hammer seeking a nail in a house that's already been built.

But art isn't necessary, either. Music isn't necessary. No one needs art or music to survive. Fine food isn't necessary. None of the castles, cathedrals, pyramids or exultant wonders of the world that men cross oceans to behold were, strictly speaking, necessary. Humans can *survive* in prisons and cardboard shanties, eating flavorless gruel, while they perform repetitive, meaningless tasks in joyless silence.

Arguments from mere utility reduce human life to its lowest and most basic form, excluding the aspects of humanity that reach beyond what is merely necessary to create the extraordinary lives, achievements, monuments, works and legacies that inspire us and spark our imaginations. They reduce us to rats in cages, monkeys, slaves.

When someone argues that masculinity is no longer necessary, what they are saying is that *your* masculinity is not necessary to *them*, and that it inconveniences or threatens them in some way, so *you* should consciously limit your potential to allow *them* to realize *their potential* or find joy and fulfillment in whatever way pleases *them*. If you confine yourself to this spiritual reservation willingly and of your own free will, you deserve the tiny, wasted life of subservience and dishonor that your owners have assigned to you.

5

Some have argued that masculinity is "artificial" or even "pathological" because it requires traumatic stimulation to develop beyond a set of inherited traits and tendencies.

For generations, feminists have been repeating their platitude that "masculinity is a mask." Masculine men have been accused of being inauthentic, and masculinity has been called "fragile," precisely because, in order for it to actualize, masculinity must be aroused, instigated and fostered. It is argued that because masculinity must be forced, and men must force themselves to be masculine, masculinity is somehow fake and all masculine men are just desperate, troubled phonies.

This line of reasoning only appeals to those who feel inconvenienced or burdened by masculinity in some way. Men who worry that they will always be found lacking by other men no matter how hard they try can comfort themselves by saying that more masculine men are just "faking it" because they are "insecure." Women who recognize that masculine hierarchical thinking is a threat to feminist egalitarian aims, or who feel dismissed or undervalued by masculine men, will naturally be inclined to emasculate and devalue them in turn by talking about how fragile, forced and "toxic" masculinity seems to be from their perspective. Bureaucracies that find themselves inconvenienced by the chaos and disruption created by masculine conflict, concerned about the possibility of violent revolt, or which simply prefer a more submissive and spinally pliable population — will also be motivated to repudiate masculinity as an artificial, outmoded and cancerous aberration.

While it is true that masculinity must be forced and fostered, this is also true of any human potentiality. One must be forced, or force oneself, to learn a language or play an instrument or solve mathematical equations. No one calls an accomplished dancer, painter, athlete or singer a phony because it took years of disciplined practice and some kind of nurturing environment for them to become what they are — for them to develop their talents to their full potential. On the contrary, to ignore these talents is considered a tragedy.

It is undeniable that, with disciplined practice, complementary nutrition, a satisfactory environment and the benefit of some knowledge gained from mentors or peers, most men can become substantially stronger and more physically capable than they would have been otherwise.

It is also true that when a man is challenged by other men on a regular basis, he will become more skilled in negotiating those challenges. When a man is continually dared to take small risks, and overcomes them, he will become more confident in his ability to take risks. When a man gets punched in the face and it isn't as bad as he thought it would be, he can proceed in life less afraid of getting punched in the face.

When a man has learned that he can master a skill, he will become more confident that he can master other skills.

When a man has made a difficult decision — done something he didn't want to do — to earn or maintain the respect, admiration and loyalty of his in-group peers, he will become more comfortable with his sense of belonging to the group, his own identity, his own principles and his ability to discipline himself according to those principles.

The tactical virtues of strength, courage, mastery and honor are "talents" — human aptitudes that are not exclusive to, but specific to masculinity and the holistic experience of being a man. To work to realize the potential of these aptitudes through disciplined practice, to seek an environment in which these potentials can be tested and fostered — this is no more artificial than working to develop any other aptitude or talent.

Determining whether developing these attributes in men is good or bad is a value judgement and that valuation depends entirely on one's interests. In making the determination as to whether or not those talents should be developed, the fact that they must be developed to flourish is irrelevant. When asking, "should a man try to become stronger," it makes no sense to say he shouldn't become stronger if he has to try.

6

In an age when masculinity is not necessary for survival, if a man wants to become better at being a man, it must be because he believes that being good at being a man is *better*.

Because he has not been coerced by external forces to choose this path, the man who chooses the way of men today is doing so of his own volition. He is choosing masculinity as a value for himself because he *wants* to. He is making a noble choice — in the Nietzschean sense — not as a reaction to external influence, but guided by his own internal sense of worthiness and the confidence in his own ability to determine what is bad, what is good, what is better, and what is best.

Unsatisfied with simply being male and inhabiting a male body, he chooses the way of men — that rigorous path toward the impossibly far North of male — to invoke and manifest within himself a higher form and a more advanced, more perfect expression of his masculine potential.

To the man who is not forced to become more masculine, but who of his own free will forces himself to seek out that route of rigor, masculinity is not a necessity, but a philosophical virtue. The word virtue itself comes from the Latin *virtus*, which roughly meant "manliness" — specifically the strength and courage-oriented martial manliness of the early Romans.

As with "honor," the conceptual volume contained within the verbal vessel of "virtue" has been expanded through a process of progressive dilution. To many, "honor" and "virtue" are synonymous with positive moral values, however they are defined by a given group in a particular context. In casual conversation, a "virtue" has come to mean almost anything any person has determined to be "good" behavior. In choosing *virtus* as a virtue, the meaning of the word "virtue" is distilled down and returned to its purest essence — virtue as virility.

The man who chooses virility as a virtue *because he wants to* has a different set of motivations than the man who is *forced* through the gauntlet of manliness by circumstance or as a matter of tradition.

The man who is forced to become stronger to survive merely did what he had to do.

The man of tradition had no choice other than to become a man — he didn't have to think much about it. The need to define and understand masculinity and articulate its virtues would seem strange to him — like someone standing up in the middle of an advanced math class and awkwardly stating that two plus two equals four.

In the countryside, in small towns, in harsh environments and on farms, some men still inherit a visceral understanding of masculinity. However, it is impossible to remain completely sheltered from the androgynous drone ethos advanced throughout The Empire of Nothing. At some point, even those few remaining men to whom masculinity seems like a default setting will have to choose a path against the estrogenic tide for themselves, or for their sons.

To *choose* the way of men independently is an intentional act of self-initiation, a voluntary spiritual path free from the demands of utility and the obligation of service. Choosing the path of strength and pressure is the act of a self-maker and self-master, a creator of values, a restless barbarian seeking what can only be found beyond the boundaries of the bare minimum.

To call out virility as a virtue — *for its own sake* — is to say, "I am a man, and that is good, because I love myself and my life and my fate and I want to be more of what I am, *for my own sake.*"

Traveling this path requires constant and conscious reflection on the nature of what man is, and what it means to become not just physically, but psychically — a more *complete* man.

(Which, of course, also implies at every point, a more complete *beast*).

THE TRAP

So, you find yourself drawn toward this perfect, unreachable star — because you recognize a dull and imperfect reflection of its light inside you. You have given value to strength, not because it is necessary or demanded of you, but because you believe that strength has value in and of itself. You have given value to strength because you love your life and love yourself and you believe that making yourself stronger also makes you more completely what you are. You have answered a call to a form, and resigned yourself to slog toward that form through an endless morass of self-imposed pain and strife.

In another age, one imagines, this striving would be expected — or widely admired at the very least.

But not this age. Today you will be called a fool and a faker. You will be lectured about the toxicity of your pursuit by partisan "experts" and you will be told, with smug and haughty snark, that your desire to become more of what you already are is a product of your "insecurity." Parroting these experts, there will be celebrities, popular writers, educators and

corporate media mouthpieces who will insist that
you are behind the times, and that you must "evolve"
— which in every instance means to become less like
a man and more like a woman. Your efforts to realize
your own masculine potential will be dismissed
with an affected amusement in an attempt to disarm
and discourage you, and in the very next breath,
the same people will say that what you are doing is
a threat to women, to "progress," to equality and to
whatever they call "freedom."[1]

*What? Did you turn this way seeking universal
affirmation?*

8

Once, the men who ruled the world commissioned
great works of art and public statues of bronze and
marble to honor war heroes as exemplars of virtue —
masculine virtue.

Today's warriors are merely memorialized as victims
of war, so that they can be regarded sympathetically
by a society in which victimhood is a marker of moral
purity and victory is morally suspect.[2]

1 I don't consider feminists "enemies." I have only contempt for
them, so further explanation of their tactics, intentions, narratives
and arguments would probably bore you — and it would just make me
feel dirty. If you are reading this, you probably already know what I am
talking about. However, I have done this dirty work in the past. For more
on mainstream anti-male feminism, read my short 2011 book, *No Man's
Land*. It is freely available online at jack-donovan.com.

2 Particularly in white masculine men, as they are the officially
acknowledged "oppressors," and one might even say "devils" — as they

Once, young males were taught about great rulers, great explorers, great inventors. They were taught the history of kings, and they were taught to be proud of the works of their ancestors.

Today, young males are taught more about the supposed evil deeds of these same great men — in the context of the prevailing morality of today, not the time in which they lived. More attention is paid to the plight of those who were conquered, or somehow treated unfairly. The "heroes" and "warriors" who have replaced the great men of history are "social justice warriors" — petulant protesters and "social organizers" who marched with megaphones for the underprivileged.

In another time, the moral arbiter of a nation or people was a king or chieftain, guided by custom and counseled by clergy, elders and advisors.

Today, who are the moral arbiters?

Corporations have far more sway over public morality than politicians, and as completely amoral profit-driven entities, they will spend millions to influence public feeling in a way that profits their shareholders and executives. As I have argued in *Becoming a Barbarian* and elsewhere, the anti-tribal, universalist ethos of the Empire of Nothing has been institutionalized primarily because it facilitates global trade, not because anti-tribalists made an overwhelmingly convincing argument.

personify moral evil in the prevailing moral system.

Still, these corporations are sensitive, jittery creatures that spasm and twist violently at the slightest change in the sediment. They are short sighted by nature, and their myriad suckers must feel their way through the daily flux of the market with a light and careful touch.

A self-proclaimed representative of any victim group can announce that they have been offended by a corporation, and no matter how absurd the nature of the offense might be, a small bandwagon of the offended, backed by a few supportive busybodies, can induce system-wide convulsions of hysteria followed by a panicked excretion of apologies and token reforms. A little bad press might give an edge to a competitor, or cause a small dip in revenue for the quarter.

Democracies defer, or pretend to defer, to the everyman — the voter. The joke is that every vote is in reality a "yes" vote that validates the options presented and the organization that presents them.

Large corporations defer to the complainer. They run a volume game, and must always be seen to be "serving" the customer - never upsetting, ignoring or excluding them.

Democratic governments, to the extent that they are still relevant, have gone the same way. Both respond to the same stimuli. Politicians must always appear to be "public servants." The quick turnaround of the 21st Century news cycle forces them to react to the ostentatiously offended with the same obfuscating squirt of desperate denial and apology. And, when they're not saying whatever they think people want to hear, they're pandering to those corporations who also pander to the offended.

In The Empire of Nothing, the high arbiters of morality are in effect the offended complainers —those grievance grifters who are always upset, always unsatisfied, always the victim, always angling for special treatment, always trying to get something for nothing.

Moral rules and social norms no longer flow from the wise or the accomplished or from custom. The new moral rules and norms and taboos are frantic mass responses to claims of discrimination, oppression, offense, hurt feelings — even a failure to affirm some obvious delusion or pathosis. Any boor who is able to throw a loud enough tantrum and make a big enough stink about some perceived slight or injustice need only attract a few cause-hopping celebrity opportunists to help them shove even the most absurd claim through the Overton window until it becomes an unquestionable norm. As long as the claim of the offended is in harmony with the all-inclusive, universalist, anti-tribal narrative of the Empire, it will likely be accepted as valid and, in time, it will be socially institutionalized. The Empire scrambles to accommodate victims, and that gives those who claim to be victims — often the most fragile, helpless, dysgenic and emotionally needy people — ultimate moral authority.

Grown men, otherwise daring, capable and virile men of accomplishment frequently find themselves terrorized and terrified by ridiculous accusations of bias or impropriety cast by spoon-fed students, indignant sluts, disabled lesbians, bipolar transsexuals, illegal immigrants and the morbidly obese.

In the space of a few hundred years, the noble morality of the sovereign has been exchanged for the ignoble morality of the squeaky wheel.

To those who have chosen virility as a virtue, who are constantly testing themselves, searching their tenacious souls daily for the tools to push forward — for reasons why they *can* and they *will* — this moral elevation of those who proudly *cannot*, who actually gain social status because they advertise that they are easily foiled, even waylaid and wounded by words alone, this turn of the worm will seem wrong... perhaps even...EVIL.

What's more, the loud losers and proud complainers will get along just fine as the administrators of their own system, and their genuflecting appeasers will very often not only praise them but place them in positions of substantial power and authority. These people who must at every turn redefine strength, courage, mastery and honor to reflect what they already are instead of what they could at the very least try to embody, these people who jealously despise masculine men, who want to redefine masculinity itself — these people will *rule* you.

They are in charge, or at the very least, the people who are actually in charge are entirely comfortable putting them in charge of *you*. They are lawmakers and judges and parole officers. The police work for them, whether they'd prefer to acknowledge it or not. Law enforcement officers may follow the way of men themselves — I know many have read the book — but they will either quit their jobs or enforce the law of the current order, no matter how perverse that law becomes. They work for the Empire.

It's easy to accept victimhood and luxuriate in it like an injured child who loves the attention. Pushing yourself toward an ideal is hard. Most people will choose the easy way if it is acceptable, and today, it is. They will learn and repeat the mantras of universal acceptance and inclusivity and shun anyone who doesn't. Most average people will allow themselves to become slobs, especially if everyone around them does, too. They will defend their "right" to be slobs, and rationalize away any opportunity to improve themselves. In the world-as-it-is and not how we might wish it to be, make no mistake — these people are normal. You beasts are the oddballs. No matter what you think of them, no matter what you do for a living, at some point you will encounter one of these perfectly normal slobs in a position where they wield power over you. Whether you want a job, or a license, or a permit, or a signature — you will have to offer the upturned paw in some way to one of these completely normal people who share none of your values.

This will be frustrating. It will be tempting to say that everything is wrong, that the world is evil, that there are fiendish degenerates ruining everything, stopping you from doing what you want to do — what you believe you should rightfully do. As you writhe and struggle on your knees, gnashing your teeth, your face red with indignation, it will be tempting to say that YOU are the victim — that YOU are the one being oppressed.

Here lies The Trap.

9

Our beast, in his quest to become more complete, comes to the realization that the ideal he has chosen to look up to has been cast down by Imperial clowns and replaced with some insane inversion of that ideal. The whole world, in fact, seems to be upside-down, crazy and ruled by the wicked. And it may seem that nothing good can be achieved until somehow, someday, the world is turned right-side-up again.

The name of this trap is RESSENTIMENT.

To continue his northward journey toward self-actualization and becoming — to become more completely what he is — our beast must break free from this trap. He must learn to recognize its insidious lures and avoid it.

But what is this, "*ressentiment?*"

In many ways it means exactly what it sounds like it means.

Resentment. Jealousy.

Ressentiment is the French version of the English word "resentment." And while it would be tempting to use the English spelling that rolls more easily off my American-born tongue, the French spelling indicates a more complex concept developed most famously by German philosopher Friedrich Nietzsche. In *The Genealogy of Morals*, he wrote:

> "The revolt of the slaves in morals begins in the very principle of ressentiment becoming creative and giving birth to values—a ressentiment experienced by creatures who, deprived as they are of the proper outlet of action, are forced to find their compensation in an imaginary revenge."[3]

Throughout his work, Nietzsche presented two moral perspectives: the outwardly justified, reactive, jealous morality of the "slave," contrasted with the confidently subjective, internally justified, proactive, noble morality of the "master."

Because I believe that the words "master" and "slave" will be distracting to many contemporary readers, and because these words are so easily taken out of context, I'm going to favor "Noble" and "Anti-Noble" from this point forward, with capitalization

---

3   Nietzsche, Friedrich. *The Genealogy of Morals* (Dover Thrift Editions) (p. 19). Dover Publications. Kindle Edition.

to identify them as specific concepts. So, when I say "Noble," I don't mean knights in shining armour saving damsels in distress or necessarily even "good" men. Or, not exactly.

The attitudes that Nietzsche associates with Noble morality are, for the most part, characteristic of an affirmative, adventuring approach to life. Noble morality is the morality, in Nietzsche's view and my own, of powerful people — of masters, conquerors and those who truly want to win and get the most out of life while they are alive. The Noble man has a great reverence and respect for strength. The Noble man *chooses his own values* because he believes in himself and his own worth and his own judgement.

For the man living in today's world, who chooses of his own volition to endure hardship not because he *hates* himself, but because he *loves* himself and wants to become stronger and realize his own potential even though his efforts are unnecessary and unwanted, I believe that Nietzsche's Noble morality offers a positive philosophical framework for self-evaluation and development. I'll expand on the Noble ideal throughout this book and specifically in the next chapter.

Anti-Noble morality is the product of ressentiment. The Anti-Noble man feels trapped. He believes that his happiness and fulfillment have been thwarted by others. He resents them for having better opportunities, for having greater wealth, for having more power, for using that power to coerce or oppress him. The Noble man views people, actions and circumstances as either being positive or negative, "good" or "un-good" in relationship to his own interests, subjectively. Instead of recognizing the tragic and unfair nature of human existence, the Anti-Noble man constructs a system of morality that he convinces himself is objective, rather than subjective — as it truly is. In the context of his worldview, the existence of his oppressor is not simply unfortunate or un-good, it is objectively, morally *evil*. Moreover, the Anti-Noble man sees himself as an innocent victim of *evil*, and believes that he himself is therefore good almost by virtue of being powerless and, he might add, being therefore uncorrupted by power. The world itself is evil, because in this world, evil men — who are evil because they have power — have power over good, innocent men who have nothing and no power.

10

Religions and ideologies that promote the renunciation of the world and all worldly things are animated primarily by this feeling of ressentiment, but they have a very broad appeal and expand successfully because the vast majority of people have very little wealth or power. And, because life isn't fair and humans are unequally gifted, even if they were given the opportunity to gain wealth and power, most people would have neither the drive nor the ability to attain or manage it effectively. Since they will never truly be powerful, it *feels* far more *empowering* for the Anti-Noble man to imagine that those who are powerful are morally evil, and that by virtue of being poor or powerless — ideally both — the Anti-Noble man is morally good. [4]

Further, whereas the Noble man says "yes" to life and seeks happiness and prosperity in the present, the Anti-Noble man has resigned himself to a happiness that can only come in the afterlife, or after the tables have been turned and the "evil," powerful people have exchanged places with the "good," powerless people. In a religious context, the good, powerless people convince themselves that they will be rewarded in Heaven, while they vengefully fantasize about the eternity of pain and suffering that their foes — the evil, powerful people — will be forced by their righteous god to endure in Hell. In a political context, the Anti-Noble man imagines "who will go to the wall" after the revolution. And, I see in many of my masculine peers, who I believe have also been trapped by ressentiment, there is a persistent fantasy of complete civilizational collapse in which the strong will survive and the weak will be helpless against the forces of chaos unless they beg the strong for protection.

"Revolution" is an interesting word to examine here, because while it has acquired a certain romantic aura, in its most basic sense, it merely implies a circular turning —like the hands of a clock or a dial, from one point in its set path of rotation to another.

---

4   This is, if there ever was one, a "morality of convenience." See also "Principles of Convenience" in my book of essays, *A Sky Without Eagles*. 2014. (Paperback Edition. Page 117.)

While I do admit that I am attracted to and inspired by the mythic poetry of cyclical history and the notion of eternal return, a more Noble approach to a desire for change is to take on the mindset of the conqueror. The conqueror creates change according to his liking, and it is good and right because he likes it — because he willed it —not because of any theoretically objective sense that it is morally good or evil. The revolutionary wants to "fix" the world by turning the moral wheel one way or the other, while the conqueror creates the world he wants.

I do not mean to imply that revolutionary political causes are necessarily Anti-Noble, or that there has never been or can never be a Noble revolution, but political upheavals tend to be uprisings that appeal primarily to the ressentiment of the masses who (rightly or wrongly) believe that they have been oppressed or mistreated by a tyrannical ruler or ruling class. Ultimately, I believe that the Nobility of a revolution can be judged by the Nobility of the culture it produces after it has "turned the knob." It is at least conceivably possible that a popular revolution could produce a Noble culture. I suppose it comes down to who ends up in charge, and how long they stay in charge.

The danger for the Noble man is in resigning himself to "wait" for the revolution.

You're alive NOW, man. *Memento mori*. Don't spend your life waiting for something to happen, for some chance occurrence, for someone else to do something for you, for someone to free you, so that you can finally be who you want to be. That's slave thinking. You might as well wait for your reward in Heaven. *Do what you can, while you can.*

In the case of the slave or the prisoner, the idea that someone is oppressing you and preventing you from living your life as you wish may be entirely accurate. Sometimes, someone may actually be keeping you down and there may be absolutely nothing you can do about it. Sometimes, things — and people — really do suck. Yet, even when this is objectively true, it is probably an unhelpful outlook. If the way of Spartacus isn't realistic, adopting the mindset of the Stoic philosopher Epictetus, who was born a slave, would probably be the next most life-affirming, self-respecting way to make the best of an undesirable situation.

Everyone faces obstacles and limitations, and ultimately it is up to you to decide what kind of man you want to be and how you are going to handle them.

11

The panicked beast, caught in the trap of ressentiment — of indignant and jealous blaming — will also feel the reflexive impulse to morally evaluate the motives and the entire ethos of the trapper. Lacking self-awareness, or perhaps suppressing it in favor of a more emotionally comforting outlook, he calls out all of the traits of the trapper and curses them. He assigns a wickedness to them, and assigns a righteousness to all of the qualities he sees in himself as one who is trapped. This is a desperate flailing about, and embarrassing to witness, but to the beast who is caught up in a vengeful fever, it is a seductively sweet delusion.

This delusion wherein the trapper is not merely at odds with the trapped, but morally evil for doing the trapping, expanded to the extent that all of the trapper's values are also morally evil — making the values of the trapped morally good by contrast — is what Nietzsche called *transvaluation*.

The inclination to transvaluate values either carelessly or neurotically in response to base feelings of envy or inadequacy is persistent and common and almost everyone does it from time to time. Each instance of transvaluation closes the jaws of the ressentiment trap and hastens the descent of the beast into reactive delusion.

Transvaluation is unnecessary and undignified and the Noble man — or the man striving to become more Noble in his conduct and character, which is the project here — should take great care to recognize and correct it in himself.

When you feel the need to argue that the things you are good at are objectively the best and most important things to be good at — to set yourself up as being more important or better than others without having to change anything about yourself — this is ressentiment-motivated transvaluation.

When you find the need to argue that the things you already do are morally superior to the things that others do — especially if they have more power or resources than you do — this is ressentiment-motivated transvaluation.

When you find the need to argue that those who have set themselves up against you are morally evil and that everything they do and believe is evil, simply because they oppose you — this is ressentiment-motivated transvaluation.

A distinction can be made between this sort of passion-based, self-elevating form of transvaluation and a more dispassionate re-evaluating of values. The motivation is what must be examined. An honest form of valuing, while still subjective, values something as an ideal because one believes it is actually better, independent of one's own attributes. The weak man who agrees that it is better to be strong — and then pushes himself to be stronger — is different from the weak man who decides strength is useless — or even morally suspect — because he doesn't have it.

Nietzsche was particularly interested in the way that the physically weak — but oh, so cunning — priestly classes colluded with the poor and downtrodden to transvaluate the values of the Noble, or knightly-aristocratic classes. Whereas the Noble classes valued strength and beauty and happiness and believed that their status was a sign of good fortune and the favor of the gods, the ascetic-priestly class taught that, "the wretched are alone the good; the poor, the weak, the lowly, are alone the good; the suffering, the needy, the sick, the loathsome, are the only ones who are pious, the only ones who are blessed, for them alone is salvation..." In contrast, they denounced the knightly-aristocratic class: "you, on the other hand, you aristocrats, you men of power, you are to all eternity the evil, the horrible, the covetous, the insatiate, the godless; eternally also shall you be the unblessed, the cursed, the damned!"[5]

In the West, Nietzsche associates this transvaluation with the influence of Christianity by way of Judaism, but he also recognizes it in other world-renouncing religions and ideologies.

The long term effect of this transvaluation identified by Nietzsche has been a complete moral inversion of the knightly-aristocratic values. What was good to them is now evil and what was bad — or contemptible — is now good. What was up, is down. What was down, is up. Ugliness is the new beauty. Weakness is the new strength. Emotional survival — endurance — is the new courage. Women are applauded no matter what they do and masculinity is institutionally denounced. Adolescents are treated as if they are supernaturally wise, and the aged and experienced are ignored or dismissed as if they were

5   Nietzsche, Friedrich. *The Genealogy of Morals* (Dover Thrift Editions) (p. 17). Dover Publications. Kindle Edition.

children. The heroes of history are now villains and every guttersnipe is glorified.

To dwell within the boundaries of this Empire of Nothing is to inhabit a space whose intellectual topography is modeled almost entirely from self-contradicting assertions, and the purpose of these assertions is to invert the meanings of powerful words.

To any man who reveres the historical cultures of knightly aristocrats and holds Noble values that are compatible with a strength-oriented ethos — the world will seem entirely upside-down.

12

Among men who are inclined to see the world as being upside-down, there are those who succumb to the trap of ressentiment. They either remain quietly stymied and frustrated — dreaming of some future righting of the world, or they set about actively blaming and scapegoating others for the sad state of things.

While it is always true that there are people to blame for the state of current affairs, as there are always people actively pushing in one direction or the other — I believe they are sometimes called "activists" — the danger here is in becoming obsessed with some "other" to the extent that you begin to determine your own values in relationship to theirs, and in the case of the Anti-Noble "other," to develop an entitled ressentiment that mirrors their own. To, in effect, set yourself up as the victim of victims.

There are also those who recognize that the transvaluation of the masculine, knightly-aristocratic values has occurred, but in their Noble desire to avoid blaming and scapegoating and to focus (admirably) on what can be done, they often fail to acknowledge the roots or the depth of that problem. They tend to paint an optimistic, rose-colored view of the challenges they face, and as a result, tend to offer inadequate solutions.

For instance, marriageable women will not magically materialize simply because men make themselves more marriageable — though they certainly will find it easier to find the few women who remain marriageable and who are willing to commit to a more traditional relationship, if that is what they desire. There are problems in the world that cannot be fixed merely by fixing oneself.

A fear of blaming and scapegoating irrationally can also lead to the development of a set of erroneous beliefs that prevent one from seeing things clearly. Refusing to evaluate something as it is because you fear the implications of that evaluation inevitably creates an error in orientation that may lead to poor decision making.[6]

---

6 See more on the "OODA Loop" and errors in decision-making in *Becoming a Barbarian* (Kindle Locations 268-288). Dissonant Hum. Kindle Edition.

Men have always complained that the generation behind them was less manly, and they have always complained that the world was going to Hell. But everything has not always been the same. The world has changed, and the values which are elevated have changed. Values fluctuate over time. Religions and ideologies come in and out of fashion, and the authorities who favor them also come and go. It is better to deal with the world exactly as it is — not as one wishes it was or believes it should be — and then make decisions realistically.

Is the world really upside-down? It certainly is, according to my own values, a "comic book dystopia." When I look around me, I see a society that is not only sick, but absurd. Ridiculous but also tragic, like a velvet painting of a sad clown. I have watched things change over my lifetime, but I have never lived in another age. We only know the distant past as a fantasy painted by historians and novelized in our own imaginations. It is impossible to know what life was really like in any particular time — or how we would fare. We are products of our own age, and can be nothing else. All we can do is hold onto that which we believe to be eternal, and believe in our own worth enough to choose values proactively, rather than reactively.

The trap of ressentiment can only be escaped with careful evaluation and calm finesse.

THE NOBLE BEAST

"[The aristocrat's system of values] acts and grows spontaneously, it merely seeks its antithesis in order to pronounce a more grateful and exultant "yes" to its own self;—its negative conception, "low," "vulgar," "bad," is merely a pale late-born foil in comparison with its positive and fundamental conception (saturated as it is with life and passion), of "we aristocrats, we good ones, we beautiful ones, we happy ones."

Friedrich Nietzsche, *The Genealogy of Morals*

Beware!

Ressentiment is the trap that can turn the noblest and most upright beast into a squirming, sniping, desperate little weasel.

But the trap is not the way. A trap is merely an obstacle along the way.

The path is not away from ressentiment, but toward a higher ideal. The Noble Beast is not traveling away from weakness, but toward strength and a lifestyle that thrives on strength. He is focused on what he is, and what he is becoming — not "others" or their paths, which serve only as warnings and counterexamples.

The Noble man values according to his own will, in the service of his own interests or — as man is an undeniably social beast — his own gang, tribe or group. He is concerned primarily with "I" and "We" — not "They." His orientation is not anti "them," but rather pro "me" or "us."

The Anti-Noble man is obsessed with the Noble man and articulates his own values by inverting the values of Nobility. The Anti-Noble man assumes that the mind of the Noble man is merely a mirror of his own jealous psyche.

However, a Noble mind is not a mirror. It is the sun.

No man is always Noble, or always Anti-Noble. Every man has a bit of the master and the slave in him — a touch of his own shadow. Like masculinity, the mindset of Nobility is an aspirational ideal that comes more naturally to some than others. It is doubtful that the most apparently Noble men *never* lapse into jealousy or blaming, or that they *never* want to curse their circumstances. It is also doubtful that Anti-Noble men are motivated *solely* by ressentiment.

It is helpful for a man who has chosen the way of men, who is striving to become a more complete man, to understand the spiritual trap of ressentiment, so that it can be recognized and avoided along the path.

But, enough about the trap, the weasel and the mirror.

Let us turn our attention, now, to the sun — to the Noble Beast himself, to the nature of this positive conception.

14

This Noble Beast is, first of all, a man.

This man was born within the physical and psychical boundaries of the Empire of Nothing, but he is possessed by an atavistic wildness. He finds himself unsatisfied with seeking only that which is necessary for his own survival and pleasure. It is a higher happiness he seeks — the joy of self-revelation and becoming that can only be achieved through pressure and trial. He loves himself, says YES to his own life, celebrates his own existence, and seeks to discharge his own strength. He is a man who wants to become more of what he is, more of what a man is. He wants to be stronger, more courageous, more skillful.

To become stronger, more courageous and more skillful he realizes that he must surround himself with and be tested by other men who demonstrate these core masculine virtues. He strives to earn the respect of his chosen tribe in word and deed, to honor them and be honored by them.

This Noble Beast has rebelled against civilization in choosing hardness over softness, in valuing what has been transvaluated, inverted and perverted by the culture of ressentiment that dominates the Empire. He has resigned himself to becoming a barbarian, an outsider, a spiritual outlaw who "wears the head of a wolf." He owes love and loyalty only to those oathed to him, who wander the outskirts of the Empire with him, shoulder-to-shoulder. He owes apologies, arguments and explanations only to his peers. He loots, plunders and pillages the Empire when it is advantageous to do so. Knowing that the Empire and its passive citizens will always align themselves against him, the outsider, he feels no remorse for those beyond the perimeter of his protection.

In this new spiritual realm, this New, Noble Barbarian — is a creator, choosing his own values and, with his brothers, he gives order to a new world within a world — remaking it from the ruins of that which came before.

These Beasts are wary of the trap of ressentiment. They recognize it, avoid it, or overcome it through honest self analysis and by seeking the constructive criticism of peers.

Because they love themselves and they look inward for value, Noble beasts see themselves as good, noble, mighty, beautiful, happy and loved by their gods. Every living thing seeks to discharge its strength, and this perception of inner worth — this strength of spirit — drives the Noble Beast to demonstrate that worth and manifest this dream of the self externally. The great joy of the Noble Beast is self-realization — characterized by a calm sense of consonance between the internal and external selves.

As a creator of values exploring a new/old realm beyond good and evil and unhindered by the "thou shalts," and "thou shalt nots" of exhausted peoples and creeds, these Noble Beasts do not perceive any desire as being wicked in and of itself, but instead rationally weigh the perceivable costs of acting on those desires against the potential benefits. These Beasts make choices as sovereigns, not penitent slaves.

The Noble Beast has the forward-facing eyes of a predator, of a beast hungry for victory and vital life. In every scenario, he looks for opportunities to win, and cannot be hindered by back-glancing thoughts of defeat or the distracting idolatry of hatred. When he encounters challenges, he "finds a way or makes one."

This Noble Beast is both creature and creator — a Dionysian man of the earth who responds to its chaos and disorder by dreaming and imposing his own solar, Apollonian vision. He is a self-creator, a visionary force of order, a starter of worlds.

15

This positive conception of the Noble Beast is not Nietzsche's "*Übermensch*," "overman," or "superman." Nietzsche was a man and a philosopher, wrestling with the ideas and problems of his own time, and he developed his own solution to those problems as he saw them from his own perspective. I am a man living in a different time, and while the problems I see are related to and in many cases prophesied by Nietzsche, they are not exactly the same. His *Übermensch* was his aspirational vision for the men of his time, and this Noble Beast, this New Barbarian, is my dream for the men of my time and the men within the perimeter of my own circle.

As careful readers will have noticed, the Noble Beast described above is a completion — or at least a filling out — of the ideas developed in *The Way of Men* and *Becoming a Barbarian*.

The Way of Men addressed the modern crisis of masculinity and outlined the four Tactical Virtues — Strength, Courage, Master and Honor. These describe how a man becomes good at being a man. These are the first values of the creative kernel of society and culture, the insular male group, the band of brothers, or what I have impishly referred to as the "gang."

One problematic criticism of Nietzsche's thought is that it often seems focused on the individual to the extent that his ideal man would not suffer the constraints of any sort of collective. He would have to rule or be alone, and that separate and atomized man — that absolute egoist and individual — ironically ends up another Last Man who, while ruler of his own mind (and even that is suspect), finds himself another tax-paying plankton floating through life at the command of that "cold monster," the state. Even self-made men and first kings, those possessed by the *regni cupido*, the "ambition of sovereignty," must bend and compromise and think beyond the "I" to the "We." *Becoming a Barbarian* addressed the challenge of thinking tribally for the lonely Western individualist — the ideal modern citizen of the anti-tribal, anti-identity "Empire of Nothing."

This Noble Beast, then, harmonically synthesizes aspects of "master morality" and the mindset Nietzsche attributes to powerful men with the tribal, masculine "barbarian" mindset that I sketched out my last two books. Elements of Nietzschean philosophy fill out a proposed philosophy of the man who wants to realize his masculine potential in a world where masculinity is "unnecessary," and Nietzsche's thoughts on the problem of ressentiment provide tools to overcome this trap and keep thinking like a conqueror instead of allowing oneself to become a scorned and hateful slave.

The next few chapters aim to develop this character sketch of the Noble Beast and inspire men to use this synthesis of Nietzsche's ideals and my own as philosophical tools to develop their "psychical power" as they venture toward that perfect,

unreachable star and become every day a little bit
more of what they are.

THE NOBLE EQUATION

"...die aristokratische Wertgleichung (gut = vornehm = mächtig = schön = glücklich = gott-geliebt)"

"...the aristocratic equation (good = noble = mighty = beautiful = happy = loved by the gods)"

Friedrich Nietzsche, *The Genealogy of Morals*

Does the serpent ask itself, "Am I *evil*?"

It strikes and discharges its venom. It devours, and it is content. It luxuriates in the summer sun until hunger inspires it to hunt again.

The serpent is wicked only to the rodent — only to its prey — who, like all creatures, values it subjectively. Both the serpent and the varmint say, "What is injurious to me is injurious in itself."[1]

---

1 Nietzsche, Friedrich. *Beyond Good and Evil* [with Biographical Introduction] (pp. 162-163). Neeland Media LLC. Kindle Edition.

In Aesop's fable concerning the Farmer and the Viper, the farmer feels pity for a freezing snake and warms it in his coat. Reinvigorated by his body heat, the viper bites the farmer, and as the farmer dies, he recognizes his error in failing to properly assess and respect the nature of the snake.

To itself, the venomous viper who hunts and strikes is surviving and thriving — heroically overcoming the adversity of the natural world by exercising its strengths and talents to the best of its ability. The serpent is the protagonist in its own narrative. He is "the good guy." For all he knew, the farmer was taking him home to make him into cowboy boots.

No beast — no matter how monstrous or terrible — would, if comparably sentient, wonder as man does, whether or not he is "evil." Evil to whom and why and according to what measure? What does "evil" have to do with living and thriving? A beast simply is what it is. It behaves according to its nature — and to the extent that animals experience what we would call "joy," it takes joy in being exactly what it is.

Nietzsche wrote that, "A living thing seeks above all to discharge its strength—life itself is will to power."[2]

This man who is most completely himself — this Noble Beast — is a beast like any other. He is motivated to live, to survive, and more important still — to THRIVE. To exert his might and display his

2 Nietzsche, Friedrich. *Beyond Good and Evil* [with Biographical Introduction] (p. 15). Neeland Media LLC. Kindle Edition.

prowess.

Without so many priestly parchments of ressentiment serving as guidebooks to distinguish the good, "god-fearing" man from the "evil" man, a man who is most completely what he is might simply say that the man who causes him pain is bad and the man who helps him or gives him gifts is good. The value of other beasts is perceived in reference to that which perpetuates or limits the individual beast's ability to survive and thrive in accordance with what it is — in accordance with its own nature.

Of course the mind of man is more complicated than the mind of the average beast, and his brain tends to sniff out and dig around in all sorts of rabbit holes looking for validation and the "meaning" of life. However, for great and powerful self-made men — men who are what they are completely, men who have oriented themselves to *conquer* — meaning and affirmation and worth must ultimately flow from within.

Why conquer, if not because you believe yourself worthy of conquering? Why fight if you don't believe you are worthy enough to win, or if you don't believe you — the living, thriving beast that is YOU — are worth fighting for? Why even bother living if you don't believe you are worthy of living well?

The man who wants to be great believes that he is worthy of greatness. And it is so because he *makes* it so.

17

Nietzsche described this internally generated sense of worth in what he called the "aristocratic value equation."

Good = Noble = Mighty = Beautiful = Happy = Loved by the Gods

Nietzsche believed that the bright, conquering people who set themselves up as nobles and aristocrats naturally assumed that they were morally good by virtue of their position of power. They believed in their own worth, and demonstrated that worth by thriving and winning and seizing the best that life had to offer them.

The noble conquerors took what they wanted, and believed that they deserved it because they were able to take it. They believed that might truly made them self-evidently right, and that those beneath them existed to support the continuation of their success and their great works.

One can even imagine a sense of *noblesse oblige* developing organically among these vigorous people, in the way that farmers and hunters develop a rational sense of stewardship over the lands and animals that sustain them. There is nothing in Nietzsche's formulation of the Noble man to suggest that he is motivated in any way by sadism or cruelty. Rather, sadism suggests a certain emotional attachment and even an underlying hatred that is more characteristic of the Anti-Noble instinct than the Noble one. There is no need to torment an animal before you slaughter it. That's unseemly, ignoble and inefficient. Likewise, a beast of burden must be tamed and disciplined in order to serve its master effectively — it must be trained — but it also makes sense to appreciate and take good care of a useful and valuable creature. No Christian commands to "love one's fellow man" or behave charitably are necessarily required to cultivate a benevolent and even appreciative relationship between what one might call "management" and "support staff."

It is not cruelty or bloodthirst or even a desire to dominate that animates the conquering soul of the Noble Beast. It is neither a hatred of weakness nor a fear of defeat. The Noble Beast is driven by dynamic self-love, and a hungry love for life. He believes that it is good to be alive, that he is fortunate to be alive, that he is blessed with the opportunity to be more fully himself, and that in becoming more fully himself, he becomes *better* and more *right*. He is as good and right and beautiful and fully alive as my dog chasing a squirrel.

The Noble Beast perceives each value listed in Nietzsche's Noble Equation as following naturally and in some way inseparable from each of the other values.

The Noble Beast believes himself to be good and noble and beautiful and happy and loved by the god — or the gods, or favored by fate — *because* he is mighty. And he believes that he is mighty and beautiful and happy because he is favored by divinity. He believes that it is good to be beautiful. Morally good. Morally RIGHT. Power and beauty are equivalent! He believes that it is good to be happy and he wants to be happier still. He wants to be better, nobler, mightier, more beautiful, happier and more favored by the gods. The Noble Beast wants MORE of everything GOOD in LIFE.

18

The Noble Equation is self-affirmative. It stands in stark contrast to the self-flagellating, self-despising, envious equation of the Anti-Noble men and women who believe that they are good because they are pious, wretched, poor, weak, lowly, suffering, needy, sick and loathsome.[3]

However, in an effort to distill the essence of nobility — especially in the context of a bourgeois age where opportunities to "conquer" or "dominate" in the purest and most primal senses are rare and limited — Nietzsche presented nobility in a way that seems likely to validate or encourage delusions of grandeur in men and women who could never claim nobility in any other way. He wrote that it is not a man's works, but his belief in his own nobility — his "reverence for himself" — that decisively characterized the nobility of his spirit.[4]

The problem with this position is that it seems to suggest that simply believing that you are "noble" or

3   Nietzsche, Friedrich. *The Genealogy of Morals* (Dover Thrift Editions) (p. 17). Dover Publications. Kindle Edition.

4   "It is not the works, but the belief which is here decisive and determines the order of rank—to employ once more an old religious formula with a new and deeper meaning—it is some fundamental certainty which a noble soul has about itself, something which is not to be sought, is not to be found, and perhaps, also, is not to be lost.—The noble soul has reverence for itself."

Nietzsche, Friedrich. *Beyond Good and Evil* [with Biographical Introduction] (p. 183). Neeland Media LLC. Kindle Edition.

"beautiful" or "powerful" actually makes you noble, beautiful or powerful. It seems to suggest that you are good and worthy of praise, no matter what you accomplish or fail to accomplish. Thinking this way may be motivating and somewhat empowering, but if you are never able to demonstrate this great worthiness you feel inside — you will become a pretentious and truly ridiculous person.

Simply believing that you are noble when you exhibit no other qualities associated with nobility does not make you noble in any meaningful way. Repeating powerful statements and bold, empty threats will not make you powerful. Unless you actually drink out of the skulls of your enemies — and you almost certainly do not — posturing as if that is even a remote possibility is some truly silly shit. You can insist that you are "beautiful," no matter how obese, slovenly or grotesque you appear to others, but doing so will not actually make you beautiful. It will make you laughable, and people should point at you and laugh.

Perhaps this problem was not so readily apparent in Nietzsche's time, but the 21st Century is characterized by an inescapable culture of feminine flattery and baseless, shameless self-affirmation. People — especially young women — are encouraged everywhere through song, film, magazines, college courses and state-sponsored health propaganda to believe and insist that they are beautiful and "amazing" just the way they are, no matter what they look like or what they do. Young men are increasingly raised by single mothers and schooled by female teachers, and they are learning to parrot these empty mantras of "empowerment." Precisely because mainstream modern culture is a culture of ressentiment in which all noble values have been transvalued, standards of beauty, strength and achievement and even health are viewed as "oppressive." It is considered offensive to question anyone's claim to beauty or brilliance or even competence — no matter how obviously absurd.

There are also members of opposing, "Traditionalist" groups who suffer from the very same problem. Having read some Julius Evola, they have convinced themselves that they are Noble "aristocrats of the soul" by virtue of believing this alone. They believe that they are superior in some spiritual sense to the multitude simply because they recognize problems in modernity and have identified themselves with a particular set of "Traditional" solutions. This absolves the "woe-is-modernity" set from having to demonstrate their nobility, and lends itself to the petulant, priestly snobbishness of the pale and baby-armed bookworm.

Believing in your own Nobility because you want to be seen as Noble, or because you want to see yourself as Noble, does not by itself make you Noble in any meaningful way. Perhaps Nietzsche recognized or resolved this when he wrote that, "...this very need of nobleness is radically different from the needs of the noble soul itself, and is in fact the eloquent and dangerous sign of the lack thereof."[5]

This intrinsic belief in one's own worth and worthiness is best seen as a starting point, a spark, a driving force. It's a recognition of potential, a recognition that one has strength to be discharged and natural desire to discharge that strength.

Keeping this in mind, here is a restatement of Nietzsche's Noble Equation better suited to our purposes:

I am clearly loved by the gods, because I was fortunate enough to be born with the potential to become mighty and beautiful and to exercise my will in such a way as to raise myself up above others. This Will-to-Power is good and right. By thus demonstrating my Nobility, I substantiate the gifts of the gods, my own goodness, and my own innate sense of self-worth. I am happy to be so blessed, and happier still when I validate these blessings through successful and vigorous ACTION.

Unless your belief in your own worth drives you to exercise your potential and demonstrate that worth, you're just another delusional loser standing in front of a mirror chanting air-headed affirmations to make yourself feel special just for being alive.

---

5 Nietzsche, Friedrich. *Beyond Good and Evil* [with Biographical Introduction] (p. 183). Neeland Media LLC. Kindle Edition.

In the words of Geoffroi de Charny, a medieval knight and exemplar of the knightly-aristocratic virtues, "*qui plus fait, mieux vault.*" He who does more is of greater worth.[6]

A high estimation of his own potential drives the Noble beast to be more, do more, to take more, to LIVE more. And the more he becomes, the more he does, the more he takes, the more he lives...the more he truly believes that he is Good, Noble, Mighty, Beautiful, Happy and Loved by the Gods...and this substantive affirmation drives and inspires him to become mightier, more beautiful and happier still. The Noble Equation is a self-affirming, self-spinning wheel of power.

19

This self-spinning wheel also spins for tribe. Each man is a spoke, venturing forward on his own linear path as a singular "one," but connected to and revolving around a central point of shared identity and purpose, with the talent and might and virtue of the group working in synergy. The belief in the worth of the self expands to include a belief in the power of the collective — of the "we." The individual recognizes the Nobility of his peers, and Noble Equation is conjugated in the third plural.

We are the Good ones, the Noble ones, the Mighty ones, the Beautiful ones, the Happy ones and *we* the

6   de Charny, Geoffroi. *A Knight's Own Book of Chivalry* (The Middle Ages Series) (p. 48). University of Pennsylvania Press. Kindle Edition.

ones who are Favored by Our Gods.

We, together, share a will to power, *we* want to exert our strength and together, *we* seek dominance. *We* want to thrive.

Modern men have been trained to be skeptical of any group that claims to be objectively "superior" to another group, because the Empire has made tribalism taboo. Still, the people in any functional group with a healthy self-conception believe, at least in some subjective way, that their group has something special going for it. Why else would anyone want to belong?

Religious sects believe they know the truth better or follow their creed better than others, activist groups believe they are morally better than others for supporting a particular cause, and sports fans somehow convince themselves that their local franchise is in some quirky way better than other sports franchises (win or lose) because it is "the home team." This tribal thinking is simply the nature of the human beast.

ACTIONS & CONSEQUENCES

The Beast who is able to escape or avoid the trap of ressentiment has moved beyond the black and white world where everything and everyone can be identified as being either "good" or "evil." Outside this realm of childlike simplicity with its tablet of rules, our Beast proceeds without a map. The Noble Beast must now weigh options and make decisions as a sovereign. He must assess his options and make the best choices possible so that he can continue to realize his potential and thrive. There is no boogeyman to blame for bad choices. Total freedom equals total responsibility.

Can you imagine a Beast so self-loathing that it berates itself — tears itself up — simply for *wanting*?

This is vice of the ignoble man, to hate himself for wanting something — for wanting *anything*. The mind of the slave who has been told "right" and "wrong" and "good" and "evil" by his master wrings his clammy hands for desiring in his heart that which his lord has forbidden him. He is a hypochondriac, constantly scanning his thoughts for the sickness of "sin."

The Noble Beast wants everything that looks delicious. He wants everything that feels good and everything that makes him feel alive. He desires freely. There is no harm in desire, no "evil" in any desire — no matter how forbidden or taboo. Wanting is free.

It is *acting* on a desire that can be expensive. Actions all have potential consequences, and when the Noble Beast decides whether or not to act, he evaluates all potential outcomes and weighs the risk of acting. No act is "evil," but the consequences may be undesirable, and if the risks of an action are high enough he may decide that acting on a desire is not in his best interest.

There is no "good" or "evil" — only actions and consequences.

21

The Noble Beast says "YES" to life, and life is RIGHT NOW. He lives and breathes and acts in the surging flux of the present tense. He is on the trek and in the game. He plans for the future, but does not *wait* for it. He remembers the past and learns from it, but he doesn't yearn for what is already gone. The Beast has no time for what "should be." What "should be" is a personal fiction, an illusion that clouds judgment. If you make decisions based on how you believe the world "should" work and how you believe people "should" behave, you will pay for it. The eyes of the Beast are clear, wet and wide open. He reacts to the actual and relies on the real. He is playing the game of life to win, and every move matters. He cannot afford to act based on what "should" happen or what would happen if the world were "better" — only what *does* happen, only what *IS*.

Men often take action to satisfy a desire without fully evaluating how that action will be perceived by others. The action itself may be simple and harmless, but the physical or social repercussions may be substantial. They may seem unfair or unreasonable or blatantly stupid. But nothing is fair and the world is unreasonable. If you cross the path of a grizzly bear to eat a handful of berries, the price of those berries may be unreasonably high, but the world doesn't care.

It is easy to confuse courage with foolishness. Self-proclaimed "rebels" say they "don't care" what people think of them, bluster that "no one is going to tell them what to do," and give a big middle finger to the world. The majority of them can soon be found complaining about the social and physical consequences of their actions, expressing frustration that the world isn't the way it "should" be. If you're going to rebel against something, decide what actually matters to you, what you are willing to sacrifice for that rebellion, avoid other unrelated rebellions, and accept the consequences of your actions with dignity. If you rebel against everything at once, you become a universal lightning rod. Good luck with that.

The law of the land is almost always unreasonable. Laws are written to satisfy all sorts of special interests that have nothing to do with your individual interests. They're as changeable and capricious as the mind of a woman and subject to all manner of mania and public whim. The case of marijuana in America is a perfect example. One year a man can go to prison for smoking or selling it, and the very next year any adult can buy it in a boutique where they sell it like wine. One must simply recognize that the law is whatever it is at a given time, and weigh the risks of breaking it. What is "good" or "evil" or "reasonable" has nothing to do with it. It all comes down to actions and consequences.

The same is true for social consequences. Today, taboos change with lightning speed. Something that was perfectly normal for a man to say or do twenty, ten, five, sometimes even one year ago can today, in mainstream circles, place one entirely beyond the pale. The Empire of Nothing is socially feminine and gossip-driven. Public discourse is dominated by the spoiled social justice "church ladies" who write clickbait. You can scream at the sky about the absurdity of this, or you can make your choices shrewdly and aim to circumvent negative consequences whenever possible. If you choose to make war with the dominant paradigm, know and accept that it will also make war with you. *Caput Gerat Lupinum.*

The law of the Empire is a grizzly to man. It's a physical reality, and if you draw its attention, there may be absolutely nothing you can do to stop it from mauling you to death. Disabuse yourself of storybook tales about your "rights." If the grizzly is hungry or angry enough, you have no "rights." History is full of stories about men who were destroyed by men who were willing to bend the rules behind closed doors for reasons of their own. The best one can do is to avoid the bear and maintain relationships with individuals who know the loopholes and can help bend the rules in your general direction.

And when it comes to social consequences, it is up to you to weigh how much the inconvenience of ignominy will restrict your movements and prevent you from becoming a more complete man, and a more complete beast.

THE CONQUERING EYE

Noble Beasts, mighty and wild, go forward always with a conquering eye! A raptor's eye, sharp and sweeping, an eye that picks out prey on the most desolate plain. An ascendent eye, undaunted by loss, always looking for the next chance to win. An eye that recognizes responsibility — but never lingers on blame — for the Noble Beast has no time for the licking of wounds.

23

The Noble Equation describes the internal world of the Noble Beast; it describes how he sees himself. Propelled by the thrust of this self-turning psychic dynamo, he sees the world before him with the savage, dilated oculus of one whose intransigent gut craves conquest before comfort and cannot be satiated in submission.

Unbound by the moral valuations of whip crackers and wary of the jealous trap, he treks through the derelict hinterland of the soul carefully and deliberately, treading lightly, evaluating the consequences of his impulses, his desires, and the choices before him with lucid reason. When he encounters challenges, he approaches them with the eye of a conqueror — the terrible and tenacious eye of a beast who looks for triumph, for some kind of win, for some positive outcome, even in his dying moment. When the way forward is blocked, his eye seeks a way around or a way through. His is the motto of Hannibal: "*Inveniam viam aut faciam.*" I shall find a way or make one.

The man who wants his hand held, who wants to be led and coddled and caressed by empty compliments — this ignoble creature encounters problems and relents. He sees only the most obvious options and is quick to make excuses. He easily resigns himself to the half-full glass. Even when adequate solutions are presented or made available to him, he prefers to question the source.

The Conquering Eye evaluates every conceivable option, and selects the one most likely to work, no matter who or where it came from, because he wants to win! The Noble Beast wants the most effective weapons, the most efficient tools, the most talented and driven people at his disposal. Consider the source, but take the best that everyone has to offer.

24

So many motivational books popular with executives and entrepreneurs simply teach people how to think like winners — like Noble, Nietzschean beasts who believe they are worthy of success and who *will* themselves to become more *powerful*. One has only to brush aside the quaint moral parsley of managerial classics to find simple and effective lessons about how to think like a man who wants to win. Examples of reactive statements like, "There's nothing I can do," "That's just the way I am," "I can't," "They won't allow that," and "If only...," are statements of the doom-and-gloom resignation that is generally accompanied by ressentiment.[1] Instead, ambitious men are encouraged to *proactively* look for alternative solutions and different approaches while controlling their own feelings and responses to challenging situations.

The Noble Beast, like the "effective" man, also approaches the world with an "abundance" mentality. He sees more than one way to win, and sees multiple opportunities for those around him to win as well. The ignoble, ineffective man sees that someone else has won, and resigns himself to being one of the losers.

25

To achieve his ends, the Noble Beast must also be willing to turn his keen eyesight inward. Not to feverishly examine himself for symptoms of festering psychological sores or constitutional handicaps — not to find excuses — but to find yet more obstacles that must be overcome. Nietzsche wrote, "The noble man honors in himself the

1 Covey, Stephen R. *The 7 Habits of Highly Effective People.* (p. 78). Free Press. 1989.

powerful one, him also who has power over himself."

Men are fond of hard and simple talk about "self-discipline," and there is something to be said for simply being able to say "no" to your own immediate desires in the service of a superordinate objective. It is also important to be able to say "no" to others, which is more difficult than it sounds to anyone who was raised to be polite and accommodating. Expansiveness is a feature of masculinity that indicates strength and security, and while cultivating the habits and image of a "despiser of rings" or a "big man in the village" can be an effective leadership strategy, it can also become something of a vice that enslaves you to obligations and a tyranny of little favors that may distract you from more meaningful achievements. One must be able to say "no" to oneself and "no" to others selectively. If you never say "no," as with women, men will never respect you, and the value of your "yes" declines economically.

The ability to say "no" to oneself is fundamental and necessary, but this sort of self-discipline is merely... disciplinary...and there's a flavor of masochism to it that one really has to have a taste for. It can be heavy-handed and oafish when applied to every situation. The Noble Beast must be able to say "no" to himself, but a man who says "yes" to life cannot thrive in a world of "no." There's a slavish craving for punishment in this. Self-control is *control*, not abstinence or asceticism. Don't love the whip too much. It is more advanced and far more interesting to learn when to say "yes" to oneself. What good is power if you never enjoy it?

To have power over oneself also means to have power over one's story. People allow their stories to control them. They write narratives about themselves based on prior experience and allow those narratives to become self-fulfilling prophecies.

There's this quote from a weird little novel by *Fight Club* author Chuck Palahniuk that's stuck with me for years and years.

> "When you realize the story you're telling is just words, then you can just crumble it up and throw your past in the trashcan."

The narrator in that particular story follows this by saying, "then we'll figure out who you're going to be."

History itself is more or less "just a story," or — especially when it comes to ancient history — a "just-so" story, written down as a parable years after events were believed to have occurred with the intent of justifying a current reality, inflating the reputation of a beloved figure or teaching a lesson. So many tales about ancient Greeks or Romans or historical figures like Ghenghis Khan are nearly unverifiable, just as "Biblical truth" is for the most part unverifiable. Most people who read these stories today are seeking some sort of inspiration or enlightenment. No one knows if Gaius Mucius

Scaevola actually put his hand in an Etruscan fire and said, "Watch, so that you know how cheap the body is to men who have their eye on great glory." No one knows if Hannibal really said, "*Inveniam viam aut faciam*" before crossing the Alps with troops and battle elephants. These stories may or may not be factually "true," but they are nevertheless inspiring.

People also retell their own stories, sometimes exaggerating their achievements with mythical pomp and flourish, but even more often, they retell these stories to explain their faults and failures. This likely increased in accordance with the deluge of pop psychotherapy which has for more than a century encouraged people to scour their own histories for signs of youthful emotional traumas that might explain their tendencies, neuroses, limitations and phobias. While it can be useful to evaluate the effectiveness and consonance of previous actions and psychological responses to events, these actions and especially one's internal responses are ordinarily as unverifiable as the details of ancient history. Unless your previous actions or responses became part of a legal proceeding or some public record, almost no one will remember them when you are dead. Almost no one actually cares about the banal minutiae of your personal story, except possibly your mother, and she has her own version anyway. You are the one keeping these stories about your past alive by repeating them to yourself and to others. Are these stories inspiring, or are they limiting?

So many obstacles in life are fictions or questionable interpretations we write about ourselves based on a belief that our past necessarily determines our future. The fact that you did something once does not mean you are doomed to do it that way again and again and again. You do not have to be who you were as a child. You don't have to be who you were in high school. You don't have to make the same mistakes, or handle things the same way that you did years ago or even yesterday.

The highest form of self-control is to stand godlike above yourself and recreate yourself according to your own will.

If your story becomes an obstacle, find a way to crumple it up and throw it in the trashcan. Focus on the present. Write a new story about how you are going to handle challenges in the future.

Many of these narratives aren't even based on past history — they're based on lack of experience, poor assessment or bad information. However, people allow these snap judgments and erroneous beliefs to limit them, because these limitations become safe and comfortable. Preemptively identifying a handicap that prevents you from doing something protects you from both the exertion and the risk of embarrassment involved in trying and failing.

People, even smart people, even people who are working hard to learn something, very often talk themselves into failing at the very thing they are working so hard to learn. The saying, "get out of your own way," applies here.

My favorite part of training with a man who is young or new to a particular discipline is recognizing that moment when he overcomes himself — when he overcomes his own narratives and instead of just forcing himself to try, he truly believes for the first time that he can. That he is capable. That he has the potential to not merely go through the motions of a thing, but to actually do well. To succeed. To do better than he ever honestly and viscerally believed that he could. That moment when he believes that he can win. When the switch flips, and a man who never truly allowed himself to believe that he could do something suddenly believes that he can — that's something special. That is a spiritual experience — an instant when his narrative has opened up and almost anything seems possible.

Seek out this transcendent moment. Control yourself not merely by saying "no," but also by challenging and conquering your own limiting narratives.

26

There is an inspiring tendency I've noticed in training alongside elite athletes, and it taught me a great deal about thinking like a winner.
Winners don't focus on losing, *even when they lose.*
I've watched men put themselves through months of grueling training, thinking every waking hour of

every day about achieving a particular goal. Then I've stood a few feet from them at the moment of truth, rooted for them and given them all of the mental support a friend can give...and watched them fail. And —minutes later — I found that I was more crushed by their defeat than they were. Often, they were already planning their training for the next event, or trying to figure out the next big goal. They weren't focused on losing, they were already looking forward the next opportunity to win. Of course they would, at some point, review their performance and try to figure out what they did wrong, but never to find excuses or someone to blame for their shortcomings — only to find opportunities to improve in the future.

We might call this tendency "golden laughter," a phrase borrowed from a passage late in Nietzsche's *Beyond Good and Evil*. He believed that Noble men were unable, "to take seriously for any length of time their enemies, their disasters, their misdeeds—that is the sign of the full strong natures who possess a superfluity of moulding plastic force, that heals completely and produces forgetfulness."[2]

The takeaway here is this: when you are tempted to luxuriate in lamentation over some loss — and we all are, occasionally — start looking instead for the next win. Shift your focus forward.

---

2 Nietzsche, Friedrich. *The Genealogy of Morals* (Dover Thrift Editions) (p. 21). Dover Publications. Kindle Edition.

27

The eye that seeks conquest cannot be distracted by hate.

The hateful eye is always looking backwards, up, around and over. The eyes of the conqueror — of the predator — are placed forward in the skull, always looking ahead. Always "on to the next one." The leery, fearful eyes of prey animals, situated on the sides of the head, scan about nervously and hatefully for the snapping jaws of oblivion. The antelope hates the lion, but if the lion hates at all, he hates only other lions.

The Noble Beast is a maker of values, a chooser of virtues, and he certainly finds those who reject or fail to live up to his high expectations to be despicable in some way. As one who believes that he is and strives to be good, noble, mighty, beautiful and loved by the gods — he holds the weak ones, the craven and crafty ones, the perpetual victims, the ugly ones and the jealous souls who seem to hate beauty itself in contempt. He dismisses them with disgust or perhaps even observes them with some small passing measure of pity. But he cannot be moved or bothered to "hate" them. He looks down upon them and hold them in low esteem.

Nietzsche wrote that, "one does not hate as long as one disesteems, but only when one esteems equal or superior."[3]

To hate is to empower and, possibly, to submit. Hatred raises up someone or some group who has "wronged" — or bested — you in some way, and bestows upon them a supernatural power and primacy in your psychic world. To hate someone is to acknowledge them as an enemy, at the very least — a dangerous equal. To hate is to honor. And, to admit that you hate some foe because they have power over you, preventing you from doing something, exerting strength and thriving — this is not only a great honor, but an upturning of the hand. It is one thing to acknowledge an unfortunate set of circumstances and even to acknowledge that these circumstances are the result of another man or group of men pressing their interests through strength or cunning, but the passion of hatred glorifies. The most poisonous insult is the bitter fruit of jealousy and ressentiment.

The best historical example of this, and I think it's worth mentioning here because Nietzsche seemed to have some conflicting opinions about it, is the question of "The Jews." While Nietzsche attributed the transvaluation of values and even ressentiment itself to some group of Jews, he also seemed to have nothing but contempt for his anti-Semitic contemporaries. I'm inclined to think he encountered in his day what I have in mine — that the men who are most obsessed with "The Jews" are

3 Nietzsche, Friedrich. *Beyond Good and Evil* [with Biographical Introduction] (p. 72). Neeland Media LLC. Kindle Edition.

the men who are most thoroughly ruled by them. These men can't stop talking about "The Jews" and ascribe fantastic, godlike powers to them that allow "The Jews" to control all things and oppress them with omniscient authority. One wonders how much better off the anti-Semites would be if they spent all of that time and energy working on improving their own circumstances or actually creating something — instead of complaining and "spreading awareness" about some Jewish conspiracy. There are small groups of Jewish activists who are obsessed with "exposing" people they call "neo-Nazis" and a small minority of white activists who are obsessed with "exposing" the "Jewish conspiracy" and I have found through experience that it is best to stay out of the way of both of them if you want to avoid the tornado of shit they both spin around them wherever they go.

It is reasonable to assess a person or a group of people and recognize that they have different or competing interests. In fact, in is reasonable to assume that almost every stranger has different and competing interests. Further, if you are not "in" a group, then that group may at some point advance interests that conflict with your interests or the interests of your own group. It is reasonable to observe the techniques and practices of other groups from a strategic perspective. This is very old and very natural — as old and natural as hunting and herding peoples competing over the best lands for hunting and grazing. This is basic human tribalism.

Hatred, however, is a distraction from winning. It's a distraction from thriving and from the enjoyment of life. There will always be circumstances beyond your control. There will always be bears in the woods. Life is never fair and it was never easy. The conquering eye looks for ways to achieve positive outcomes in negative situations.

Hatred is a form of spiritual exhaustion, a passive masochism that relaxes into impotent submission when a man or a people have spent their will-to-power and creative energy resigning themselves to a purgatory of blame-seeking and comforting excuses. To escape the black gravity of this purgatory, the impulse to blame and hate must be overcome and replaced with the fire of visionary creativity and a renewed passion for life.

CREATURE AND CREATOR

"The tension of soul in misfortune which communicates to it its energy, its shuddering in view of rack and ruin, its inventiveness and bravery in undergoing, enduring, interpreting, and exploiting misfortune, and whatever depth, mystery, disguise, spirit, artifice, or greatness has been bestowed upon the soul—has it not been bestowed through suffering, through the discipline of great suffering? In man creature and creator are united: in man there is not only matter, shred, excess, clay, mire, folly, chaos; but there is also the creator, the sculptor, the hardness of the hammer, the divinity of the spectator, and the seventh day—do ye understand this contrast?"

Friedrich Nietzsche, *Beyond Good and Evil*

Man is a creature who has the *potential* to become a creator.

However, to be good at being a man — to manifest, demonstrate and embody the virtues that men

recognize immediately as masculinity in each other — it is not necessary to create or even to procreate.
How many brave warriors — bold and brilliant exemplars of Strength, Courage, Mastery and Honor — have died childless on the battlefields of history? How many men who were shrinking, delicate, embarrassments to their brothers have managed to seed a woman? One can be good at being a man without becoming a father, and one can become a father without ever being very good at being a man.

Man has the *potential* to create his world, to dream cosmologically and ejaculate his vision upon the womb of the earth, to call up that creation from the fertile soil as the sun calls the trees toward the sky. Man is capable of reordering and reshaping the world around him to please him and to serve him. From simple stone, he can bring forth swords and statuary, pillars and Parthenons. Man can give names and meanings, and in this naming, reorient the perceptions of other men. Man can tell a story or paint a picture that propagates in the minds of men and women he may never meet. Man can look upon his peers and organize them into a priesthood, a band of pirates, a congress, a round table, or a regiment. What is all of this, if not magic? This visionary potential to make and to master — this is the spark of a god in man!

But, to be good at being a man, as a beast, this creativity is not required. A man can be strong, brave, competent and beloved by his brothers without ever creating much of anything.

To be good at being a man in any time is good enough for most, and to strive to be better at being a man in this flabby, flaccid and feminine age is an upstream slog worthy of a solid nod. Even this, I would argue, is a creative act. There is something different in the man who makes that choice which distinguishes him from the man who allows himself to be swept along with the current. This man, at the very least, is a self-creator and a chooser of values.

There are many virtues that we could identify and encourage in men. Philosophers and theologians and football coaches have come up with countless lists of masculine virtues and values. The task of weeding through these lists to separate the aspects of the masculine experience that were both universal and essential produced the four Tactical Virtues of masculinity. Most of the others serve a particular society or culture or worldview, or are "too human" and not specific enough to men or masculinity. However, if I were to suggest an optional fifth virtue of masculinity that, while not always required to be perceived as being good at being a man, is still profoundly relevant to the experience of maleness, that virtue would be "Creation."

Throughout history, humans have recognized and revered the generative power in man. This is symbolized, most obviously, by man's procreative potential and the sexual act.

Woman, the fertile earth, waits. Perhaps she even lures or coaxes, as she serves her own ends. However, to *conceive* human life — the word "conceive" itself comes from a root that means "to take" — woman relies on male *action*. Male procreative action *initiates* life, *gives* life — *starts a new human world.*

To be a human male whose body is functioning properly is to experience sexual desire and the impulse toward carnal creation, even if that desire is intellectualized, suppressed or diverted in some non-reproductive way. This impulse toward biological creation is a universal male experience that has made male sexuality a powerful metaphor for more abstract creative activity.

The sex act itself is the act of man as a beast, satisfying his primal desire. Despite desperate attempts to sanitize it by clammy, life-despising puritans and efforts to elevate and decorate it with charming euphemisms about "love-making," despite all of the hand-rubbing double-talk of sleazy spiritual gurus — at the moment of climax, sex is the chthonic convulsion of a creature overcome by the wild darkness of nature. At no moment are we more nakedly — more *completely* — beasts.
And yet, this feral rutting toward insemination and oblivion also symbolizes the potential in man that exists in no other animal. All animals reproduce themselves. Man can also reproduce his dreams.

Dreaming alone is unremarkable, but when man takes action and imposes his dream on the world around him, he realizes a potential in himself that differentiates him from simpler men and beasts. It is this visionary creation — facilitated by the strength and the will to impose it! — that distinguishes the Noble beast who masters the world around him from the average beast. It is through visionary creation that man truly becomes what he is and completes himself. Visionary creativity is not necessary to be good at being a man, but it is what separates *great* and *Noble* men from other men.

29

Where are you, creators? Noble beasts? Where are the men of the wheel and the chariot, the terrors of the steppe, the men of thunder and the shining sun? Where are the men who make marvels and masterpieces, who found orders and demand not merely utility — but beauty? Who has a symphony in his heart? Where are the egos big enough to build castles? Who among you has the courage to become a new prophet for a new age? Better still, a thousand new prophets for a thousand new ages! Only YOU can drown out the mind-numbing hum of the universal hive!

I know that not all of you can become or even want to become "Zarathustra." Not every man is concerned with being great, but if you're reading this, you're reading it because you want to be greater. You want to become better. You want to access the potential that you have and become the best version of yourself. You see all of the problems in the world that I see, but you want to overcome them and *thrive* despite them, because you love yourself and you love being a man and you want to discharge your strength and LIVE while you are alive.

This manly beast, in his savage completeness, walks the earth without remorse for his existence. He is unconcerned with external sources of moral valuation, because he believes in his own judgement and his own worth. However, he is a social beast, when he walks with others, he must consider the consequences of his actions and judgements on the group. He is hungry for victory, always moving and looking forward, searching for the next feast and demonstration of his worth — always looking for the next win.

The mindset of this complete beast — this Noble creature — is, in itself, a solution to navigating the challenges of this comic and dystopic wilderness and avoiding the trap that turns men of worth into weasels. The spiritual path that leads beyond that land of waste is the path of creation. Creation is the countermeasure to blaming and complaining, resentment and resignation. Beyond even overcoming, creation is positive action in the opposite direction of ressentiment. The creator makes not only the way, but the world. Creation is the distinguishing characteristic of Nobility. Masters redefine and reshape the world around them. This is the true way of first kings and the kernel of aristocracy — conquering is the successful discharge of strength, but creation is the imposing of will and vision. In the vacuous wake of melee, the Noble Beast reorders his world. This is the work of a

Romulus.

Today, the men who value Strength, Courage, Mastery and Honor — the men who love being men and who want to be more of what they are — tend to become frustrated, angry and reactionary. I understand these frustrations and I understand the anger, but you can't turn back the clock and return to some idealized version of the past. The future is all that you have ahead of you, and the best way to improve your own life is to create a positive vision for your own future and begin to shape the world around you. Maybe that means procreating and focusing on raising a family, maybe it means creating or helping to create an organization or a work of art. Maybe it means investing in your career or running a business that allows you to become a patron and fund new art and new culture that is in harmony with your own aesthetic and philosophical values. If you're angry at the media, *create your own.* If your channels are being shut down, make new channels. Be the visionary father and *make the way.*

30

Nietzsche theorized that the Ancient Greeks were, "obliged to create" both great art and the Olympian gods themselves out of necessity, as a response to suffering, chaos and disorder.[1] He believed that their highest art form was Attic tragedy, specifically the work of Aeschylus and Sophocles, and in that drama

1   Nietzsche, Friedrich. *The Birth of Tragedy* (Oxford World's Classics) (p. 28). OUP Oxford. Kindle Edition.

he saw a controlled tension between what he called the Apollonian and the Dionysian elements in man. The Dionysian, named for the Greek god of wine, was symbolized by the chorus, chanting and singing in unison. The Dionysian force is the creature in man — earthy, intoxicated, lusty, impulsive, lost in the undulating, unified consciousness of the eternal. Apollo is the god of the sun, and of prophecy. Nietzsche associates him with "the plastic arts," including sculpture and even poetry. The Apollonian reacts to Dionysian disorder by dreaming his own world into existence, by giving it shape and putting it in order.

This theory that the principle mechanism of creation relies on an exchange between visceral, mysterious darkness and the light from the sky that reveals order is even older than the Greeks. It's an echoing theme that runs through Indo-European culture and religion. Linguists and archaeologists have reconstructed a skeletal sketch of Proto-Indo-European mythology and religion from its surviving cognates.

Proto-Indo-European is believed to have thrived in the Pontic-Caspian steppe between the fifth and fourth millennium BC, and is regarded as the root language and culture that produced the earliest forms of Western, Slavic, Persian and Indic languages — including English, German, Latin, Greek, Spanish, French, Russian and Hindustani.

The Proto-Indo-Europeans believed that, at the beginning of time, there was a pair of twin brothers named *Manu and *Yemo, accompanied by a cow. *Manu (the root of the word "man"), sacrificed his brother *Yemo (which may mean "twin"). Assisted by the sky gods, *Manu made the world from the parts of his brother's dismembered body. *Manu "became the first priest, the creator of the ritual of sacrifice that was the root of world order."[2]

The sky gods who assist or bless his creation — or in honor of whom his sacrifice was made — are *Dyeus Ph₂ter, the "sky father," and *Perkwunos, the god of war and the storm. Dyeus, or "sky," became the word for god itself, as in Deus, Dios, *Tîwaz and the Indo-Aryan deva. His characteristics, blended with the power of warrior-god *Perkwunos, are found in the Greek Zeus and the Roman Jupiter. The thunder of the storm god reverberates in Thor, Indra and the Slavic Perun. There are remarkable similarities concerning the theme of creation through bloody sacrifice in hymns of the Rig Veda[3] and in the Germanic cosmology in which the world is crafted from the slain body of Ymir by Odin — who inhabits an Olympian sky-realm above and beyond humanity known as Asgard.

---

2   Anthony, David W.. The Horse, the Wheel, and Language: How Bronze-Age Riders from the Eurasian Steppes Shaped the Modern World (Kindle Locations 2498-2503). Princeton University Press. Kindle Edition.

3   Doniger, Wendy. The Rig Veda (Penguin Classics) (pp. 29-31). Penguin Books Ltd. Kindle Edition. See 10.90 Purusa-Sūkta, or The Hymn of Man

As god of madness and inspiration, in addition to being the sky-dwelling Allfather and visionary creator, Odin incorporates the Dionysian and the Apollonian — the chthonic and the solar elements of creation — into one god-concept. It is possible that the later, more thoroughly recorded tales of Odin found in the Eddas may have combined aspects of the calm, rational and solar Tyr or *Tîwaz* with the wild, magical, ecstatic aspects of Odin or *Wôdhanaz*, eventually assigning Tyr a supporting role.

Still, as comparative philologist Georges Dumézil pointed out in *Mitra-Varuna*, the "one-eyed god" and the "one-handed god" together still symbolize another collaborative duality found throughout Indo-European ideas about the nature of creation and leadership. Tyr sacrificed his hand to make the gods' binding of the terrible wolf Fenrir a balanced legal agreement, whereas Odin sacrificed his eye for mysterious wisdom. Dumézil also noted that early forms of Tyr (*Mars Thincsus*) presided over the "thing" —the gathering during which Germanic tribal societies decided important legal and official matters. This dark-light dualistic collaboration between the "magician" and "jurist," between the "terrible" and the "ordered," is another facet of the dark/light, earth/sky dynamic that Dumézil found in the Roman kings Romulus and Numa, as well as the Indo-Iranian pairing of Mitra and Varuna. The sober and rational arrangement of creation proceeds from the wild mystery of inspiration, unreason and intoxication.

31

It is through this solar reaction to darkness and chaos that the creature of man becomes a creator and seeds the Dionysian earth with his Apollonian dreams. The beast of man is of the earth and its wet, eternal mystery pulses just beneath his skin, but he accesses his greatest potential — his nobility and godhood — when he commands it and gives it shape, first in his dreams, and then by mastering himself and the world beyond himself. The base creature, when cornered, lashes out wildly in the dark. The Noble Beast — man in his completeness — rises and lights up the night with the solar vision of a bold creator.

Oh, you reactionaries...

I know your anger and your suffering. I know the star that calls you and in following that star I too have stumbled into the trap of ressentiment. Of blaming and hating and screaming at the sky. I've been blocked by the dense wood and I see the towering wall of stone, but...

...greatness flows from the creativity and overcoming that chaos and challenge inspires in the man whose Noble belief in his own worth drives him forward to demonstrate his potential and realize the miracle of his own godhood.

If you cannot see the way, make the way.

If you despise the world around you, do not lament the passing of a dream you never knew — dream the world that you want NOW. Begin from where you are. Dream a new world and impose it from above. Thrust your hands into the decaying soil, scoop it up and sculpt it — give it shape with all of your strength. Life was never fair and creation was never easy. Take the world you have and make the one you want. Be the god that gives it life.

And if you don't know where to start — if you have nothing but your own body — start there. Create and recreate yourself. Be the clay, and become your own dream. Not because you have to, or because it is needed or necessary, but because you want to.

Why not?

Isn't that what the conqueror, the master and the first king says?

"Why not me?"

Why not be the creature who creates himself?

And...then...

ACKNOWLEDGEMENTS

A spark for this book came from a conversation with a friend who we will call "Gunnar." In response to various concerns about the lying press and the obstacles associated with saying anything controversial at all, Gunnar said to me, "The solution to all of these problems is creation." And I agreed. Good one, Gunnar. Thanks.

Along those lines, I'd also to thank all of my other brothers who have worked together with me, challenged me, and inspired me over the last few years.

:AR:A:HARI:

HTW!

ABOUT THE ARTWORK

CREATURE AND CREATOR

The two symbols I created for this book are both derived from a Bronze Age sun wheel pendant originally found in Zürich, and dated to the 2nd Millennium B.C. I was drawn to this particular design because it represents an ancient and authentic connection to the continuity of solar symbols that extends through Indo-European cultures all the way back to their theoretical source in the Pontic-Caspian Steppe. The sun wheel, sun cross, or *Sonnenkreuz* symbolizes not only the sun, but motion and momentum, turning and action — referencing the invention of the spoked wheel and the terrible glory of the battle chariot.

On the cover art, a sharp-toothed skull screams out across time, with his third eye open, symbolizing the beast of man engaged in visionary creativity, godlike, imposing a dream of order from above.

SOLAR VISION

The Solar Vision symbol is a more compact and reproducible rendition of the same concept. The original solar wheel is more apparent, and the solar cross is completed in center of the visionary eye.

Lightning Source UK Ltd.
Milton Keynes UK
UKHW01f1857250918
329518UK00002B/330/P